ROCKS & MINERALS

SEYMOUR SIMON

HARPER

An Imprint of HarperCollins*Publishers*

To Liz Nealon, my wife and helpmate

Special thanks to Bob Byrne

PHOTO CREDITS

Page 3: © Liz Nealon; page 4: © Naeblys/Shutterstock; page 6, top to bottom: © MonumentalArt/Shutterstock; © Madlen/Shutterstock; page 7: paulrommer/Shutterstock; page 8: © Nastya22/Shutterstock; page 9: © Yury Kosourov/ Shutterstock; page 10: © nantarpats/Shutterstock; page 11, top to bottom: © Dirk Wiersma /Science Source; © vvoennyy/123rF; page 13: © Anneka/Shutterstock; page 14: © Igor Masin/Shutterstock; page 15, top left to bottom right: © Ingemar Magnusson/Dreamstime.com; © Alexander Maksimov/Dreamstime.com; © Dario Lo Presti/Dreamstime.com; © Ingemar Magnusson/Dreamstime.com; page 16: © Albert Russ/Shutterstock; page 17: © Howard Edin; pages 18–19: © www.sandatlas.org/Shutterstock; page 20: © Zelenskaya/Shutterstock; page 21: © tamsindove/Shutterstock; page 22: © Suphachok Rengsomboon/Shutterstock; page 23: © Martin M303/Shutterstock; page 24, top to bottom: © Renewer/ Shutterstock; © kavring/Shutterstock; page 25: © Tom Grundy/Shutterstock; page 26, top to bottom: © Tatiana Popova/ Shutterstock; © vvoe/Shutterstock; page 27: © Ambient Ideas/Shutterstock; page 28: © hecke61/Shutterstock; page 29, left to right: © www.sandatlas.org/Shutterstock; © vvoe/Shutterstock; © www.sandatlas.org/Shutterstock; page 30, left to right: © Foto-Ruhrgebiet/Shutterstock; © Albert Russ/Shutterstock; © Mark Steinmetz; page 31: © Mark Steinmetz; page 32: © Albert Russ/Shutterstock; page 33, top to bottom: © Nastya22/Shutterstock; © Igor Masin/ Shutterstock; © farbled/Shutterstock; © Nastya Pirieva/Shutterstock; pages 34–35: © Peter Kim/Shutterstock; pages 36–37, left to right: © Nastya Pirieva/Shutterstock; © Albert Russ/Shutterstock; © RATCHANAT BUA-NGERN/ Shutterstock; © ANKA Nikolova/123RF; © Ingemar Magnusson/123RF; © vvoe/Shutterstock; © Nastya22/Shutterstock; © photographieundmehr/123RF; © Domiciano Pablo Romero Franco/Dreamstime.com; © Igor Masin/Shutterstock; page 39: Tammy Bryngelson/Getty Images; page 40: © Cultura Limited; page 42: © Valentin Gaina/Shutterstock; pages 44–45: © Nico Muller Art/Shutterstock; page 46, top left to bottom right: © Albert Russ/Shutterstock; © Madlen/ Shutterstock; © Nastya22/Shutterstock; © Yury Kosourov/Shutterstock; © vvoennyy/123rF; © RATCHANAT BUA-NGERN/Shutterstock; © Igor Masin/Shutterstock; © Ingemar Magnusson/Dreamstime.com; © Alexander Maksimov/ Dreamstime.com; © Dario Lo Presti/Dreamstime.com; © Ingemar Magnusson/Dreamstime.com; © Thorsten Schmitt/ Shutterstock; © www.sandatlas.org/Shutterstock; © Renewer/Shutterstock; © kavring/Shutterstock; © farbled/ Shutterstock; page 47, top left to bottom right: © Tyler Boyes/Shutterstock; © Tatiana Popova/Shutterstock; © Anneka/ Shutterstock; © vvoe/Shutterstock; © vvoe/Shutterstock; © www.sandatlas.org/Shutterstock; © www.sandatlas.org/ Shutterstock; © Nastya Pirieva/Shutterstock; © Foto-Ruhrgebiet/Shutterstock; © ANKA Nikolova/123RF; © Ingemar Magnusson/123RF; © photographieundmehr/123RF; © Domiciano Pablo Romero Franco/Dreamstime.com; © Albert Russ/Shutterstock; © Tom Grundy/Shutterstock; © Albert Russ/Shutterstock.

Rocks & Minerals

Library of Congress Control Number: 2016940931
ISBN 978-0-06-228918-6 (trade bdg.) — ISBN 978-0-06-228917-9 (pbk.)

17 18 19 20 21   SCP   10 9 8 7 6 5 4 3 2 1

❖

First Edition

Author's Note

From a young age, I was interested in animals, space, my surroundings—all the natural sciences. When I was a teenager, I became the president of a nationwide junior astronomy club with a thousand members. After college, I became a classroom teacher for nearly twenty-five years while also writing articles and books for children on science and nature even before I became a full-time writer. My experience as a teacher gives me the ability to understand how to reach my young readers and get them interested in the world around us.

I've written more than 300 books, and I've thought a lot about different ways to encourage interest in the natural world, as well as how to show the joys of nonfiction. When I write, I use comparisons to help explain unfamiliar ideas, complex concepts, and impossibly large numbers. I try to engage your senses and imagination to set the scene and to make science fun. For example, in *Penguins*, I emphasize the playful nature of these creatures on the very first page by mentioning how penguins excel at swimming and diving. I use strong verbs to enhance understanding. I make use of descriptive detail and ask questions that anticipate what you may be thinking (sometimes right at the start of the book).

Many of my books are photo-essays, which use extraordinary photographs to amplify and expand the text, creating different and engaging ways of exploring nonfiction. You'll also find a glossary, an index, and website and research recommendations in most of my books, which make them ideal for enhancing your reading and learning experience. As William Blake wrote in his poem, I want my readers "to see a world in a grain of sand, / And a heaven in a wild flower, / Hold infinity in the palm of your hand, / And eternity in an hour."

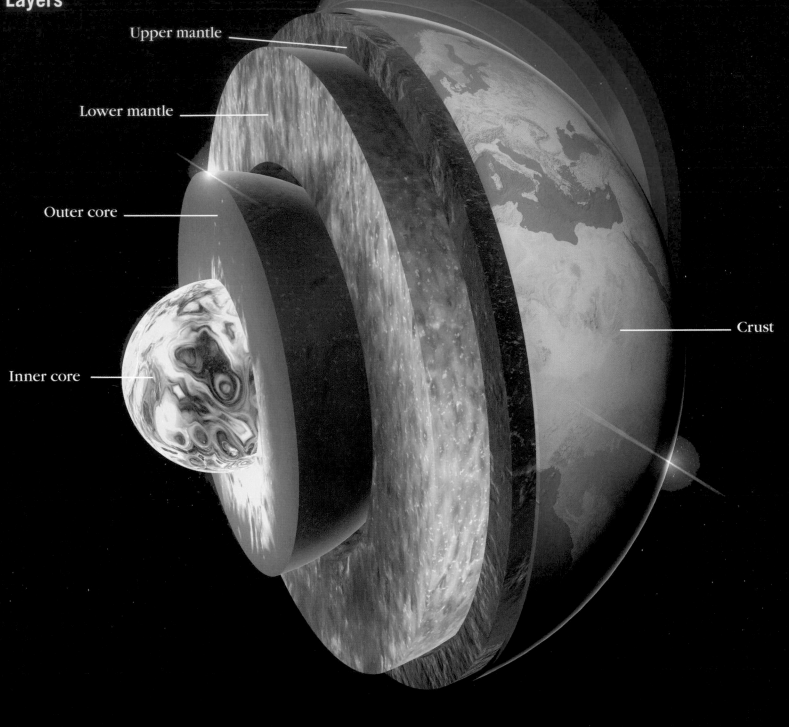

The Structure of the Earth
Layers

Upper mantle

Lower mantle

Outer core

Inner core

Crust

You live on the top solid layer of our planet Earth—the **crust**. Earth's crust is like the skin of an apple. It's very thin compared to the other layers that make up Earth. Earth's crust is only about 4 miles (6 kilometers) thick under the oceans and about 25 miles (32 km) thick under the continents. Underneath the crust is a 2000-mile-thick layer of rock called the **mantle**. Below the mantle is a 2000-mile-thick **core** made up mostly of iron and nickel. The core is divided into two different zones, a molten outer core and a solid inner core.

The crust contains many different kinds of rocks and **minerals**, such as granite, sandstone, basalt, quartz, and mica. No matter where you walk, in your neighborhood or in a distant land, you can find rocks and minerals on the crust. Rocks and minerals on the crust are clues to what happened millions and millions of years ago in Earth's history. They tell us about long-ago volcanoes, mountains, and oceans.

Scientists, called **geologists**, find and study rocks and minerals to try to solve the mysteries of Earth's past. You too can find and collect rocks. You can become a **rock hound**, someone who collects and builds a collection of different kinds of rocks. This book is for beginning rock hounds, but it is not just for reading. It's an invitation to go out and explore the world of rocks and minerals.

Minerals are made up of chemical substances called elements. Ninety-two different elements are found in nature. Only about ten elements, such as gold, copper, and carbon, have been found in a pure form. All the other minerals are

Amethyst

combinations of elements called **compounds**. There are about five thousand different kinds of minerals that have been found so far.

Many minerals form in the shape of beautiful **crystals**. Crystals are definite shapes, such as a cube or a pyramid, that look different for each mineral. For example, quartz crystals always look different from pyrite crystals. In fact, you can identify a mineral by the shape of its crystals. Large crystals are rare; most crystals that you find are fairly small.

Malachite

Crystals are a special shape that forms

when the molecules of a mineral fit together in a repeating pattern. Minerals form crystals when **magma**, or molten rock, cools slowly. No two crystals are exactly alike—some are as big as your hand, others are as big as your leg, and still others are tiny enough for you to need a magnifying lens or even a microscope to see. But crystals formed from the same type of mineral look alike. For example, garnet crystals have the same shape whether they are big or small. Some minerals have several shapes. Pyrite forms crystals that are either cube shaped or have twelve sides. One of the more interesting shapes that some minerals form is a needlelike mass of radiating thin crystals. Minerals that form these kinds of crystals include gypsum, rutile, and malachite. These crystals are easily broken and it's rare to find them in nature.

Gypsum

Here are some of the most common minerals that you are most likely to find in nature.

Quartz is the most common mineral on Earth. It is found in many different kinds of rocks, including granite, schist, and gneiss (pronounced *nice*). Beach sand is mostly finely ground quartz. You can also find quartz in pure crystal form, sometimes in cracks in rocks, other times within a hollow rock ball called a geode. Quartz may come in many different colors, and its **luster** varies from glassy to waxy. Quartz can be used to scratch glass and cannot be scratched by a steel knife. Colored kinds of quartz such as amethyst and rose quartz are **semiprecious** and are used in jewelry.

Quartz

Feldspar

Feldspar is the name for a group of minerals similar to each other. Quartz is more common than any single feldspar, but all the feldspars taken together are five times more common than quartz. Feldspars are hard enough to scratch glass but not quite as hard as quartz. Feldspars range from glassy to pearly in luster. Feldspars break in right-angled pieces, unlike quartz, and that's about the best way to tell them apart. Don't worry about trying to identify each kind of feldspar; just try to tell them apart from quartz.

Calcite is found in many different rocks. Next to quartz, it's the most common single mineral. It's the main mineral in limestone and marble. It's also the mineral that creates stalactites and stalagmites, icicle-like forms found in caves in limestone areas. Calcite is very soft and can be scratched with a penny. Another way to identify calcite is to scrape a piece into a powder and put a drop of vinegar (a weak acid) on it. The calcite and vinegar will bubble rapidly.

White is the most common color of calcite, but it can also be pale shades of pink, blue, green, yellow, or even clear. Clear calcite, such as Iceland spar, looks like glass but has a fascinating optical property. Place a piece of Iceland spar over a printed page in a book or newspaper. You'll see the text doubled. Calcite bends light waves in such a way that anything seen through the transparent crystal looks double.

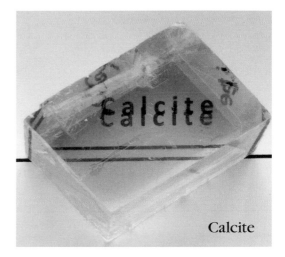
Calcite

Mica is not a single mineral but, like feldspar, is a group of related minerals. Mica is easily recognized. It peels apart into flat, smooth sheets. If you find a large piece of mica, you can easily peel it into sheets thinner than the pages of a book. Mica is very soft and can be scratched with your fingernail. Mica is found in rocks such as granite, gneiss, and mica schist. You can recognize it by the tiny flakes that glitter as you turn the rock around in sunlight. Mica flakes are often used as artificial snow in window displays. Mica is also used in many ways in industry, such as an electrical insulator and as a planting medium for seeds.

Mica

Other properties may help you to identify some minerals. For example, some minerals, such as magnetite, are attracted by a magnet. Certain rare minerals even have a particular taste or odor.

Minerals also differ in their specific gravity, or their weight compared to the weight of an equal amount of water. Gold, for example, has a specific gravity of 19. That means that a piece of gold is about 19 times heavier than an equal amount of water. Quartz has a specific gravity of only 1½. That means that a piece of gold is much heavier than a piece of quartz of the same size.

Some mineral crystals are called gems. Gems, such as diamonds, emeralds, rubies, and sapphires, are cut and polished and look beautiful in jewelry. These are rare and expensive. Many other gems, such as garnets, amethysts, and opals, are beautiful in jewelry but not so rare. These are sometimes called semiprecious gems. Many gems are very hard and do not scratch easily.

There are certain minerals that glow in beautiful colors in a dark room under a special kind of lamp that gives off ultraviolet rays. The glow of a mineral under ultraviolet light is called fluorescence. Willemite, autunite, and some kinds of calcite are fluorescent. Never look directly into an ultraviolet lamp; it can be dangerous for your eyes.

Citrine

Jasper

Peridot

Chalcedony

Amethyst

Rock crystal

Olivine

Smoky quartz

Malachite

scratch a diamond. Diamond is also the best conductor of heat, so when you touch a diamond at room temperature it feels cold because it conducts heat away from your fingers. When diamonds are cut or faceted, they look shiny and brilliant. Diamonds range from colorless through yellow and brown, to pink, green, blue, and, rarely, even red.

Emeralds and aquamarines are crystals of a mineral called beryl. Pure beryl is colorless, but even a small amount of an impurity turns beryl into a gem mineral. Emeralds are green and aquamarines are blue, but other beryl gems can be pink, yellow, or blue-green.

Emerald   Aquamarine

Meteorite

Rocks are solid parts of Earth's crust made up of one or more minerals. Only about thirty minerals are called rock-forming minerals. They make up almost all the rocks you may find. But there are thousands of different kinds of rocks on Earth. There are rocks of all colors—red, green, white, black, yellow, and blue. There are smooth rocks and rough rocks, shiny and dull rocks, rocks made up of one mineral and rocks made up of many minerals. Rocks can come from space too. They are called **meteors** when you see them flame across the night sky and **meteorites** if they land on Earth before burning up in the atmosphere. About fifty thousand years ago, an enormous meteorite made the more than half-mile wide Meteor Crater in Arizona. The space rock weighed 300,000 tons. When it crashed on the ground, it exploded with a force 150 times greater than an atomic bomb. But most meteorites are small, no bigger than pebbles. You might have a hard time identifying a small meteorite, as it looks like a lump of blackened rock. It's only when it is cut and viewed under a microscope that a scientist can tell you what it is.

Kilauea lava flow

Obsidian formed by lava

How can you make sense of all these rocks? Rocks can be grouped together in many different ways. You can group them by their color, by the minerals they contain, by their hardness, or by how they are used by people. But most of the time, rocks are grouped together by the way in which they were formed in Earth's crust. According to this method of grouping rocks, the three main types of rocks are igneous, sedimentary, and metamorphic.

Igneous rocks are formed by the cooling and hardening of hot, molten rock from within Earth's crust and upper mantle. The word *igneous* means having to do with fire. The hot molten rock within Earth is called magma. When it erupts on the surface of a volcano it is called **lava**. Igneous rocks are the first kinds of rocks that appeared on Earth's surface.

Granite

The most common kind of igneous rock is granite. You can find pieces of granite almost anywhere you look. Granite has large grains of the minerals quartz, feldspar, and mica. Granite forms when molten magma cools slowly deep inside Earth. The colors vary from gray to tan to red depending upon the other minerals present in the rock, but granite is usually speckled because of the large grains of minerals that make it up.

Other kinds of igneous rocks are gabbro, basalt, pitchstone, and obsidian. Gabbro is a dark speckled rock with coarse crystals of minerals such as olivine, augite, and magnetite. The large crystals form when magma cools slowly. When gabbro is thinly sliced by a rock cutter, the crystals may show up beautifully under a microscope. Layered gabbro has alternate layers of dark and light minerals.

Basalt is a dark rock formed by lava that cools more quickly. It is similar to gabbro but has much finer grains or crystals. When basaltic lava cools, it sometimes splits into large, six-sided pieces of rock that look like a strange pathway along the ground, such as with the basaltic columns that make up the Giant's Causeway in Northern Ireland.

Pitchstone and obsidian are igneous rocks that may also form when lava cools quickly. Both are dark rocks, but pitchstone is a dull, rough rock, while obsidian is a shiny, smooth, usually black rock that looks like glass. Obsidian is a hard rock that forms very sharp edges when you break it; because of this, ancient people often used pieces of obsidian as cutting tools.

The Giant's Causeway, Antrim, Northern Ireland

Dinosaur footprint

Sedimentary rocks come from other rocks and minerals that were worn down or dissolved in water. Rocks are worn down, or eroded, by wind, running water, heat, and cold. The little pieces of worn-down rock are called sediments, and they settle on the bottom of the ocean or roll downward from hills and mountains. Sediments are also carried along by rivers and other bodies of running water.

Over the years, more and more sediments are deposited on low-lying places. As the older layers are buried, the new sediments squeeze and compress them with their weight. The layers of loose sediments harden and become more compact. Over many thousands of years, the sediments turn into rocks such as limestone and sandstone. Limestone may contain the fossilized remains of once-living creatures, some with shells. Chalk is a kind of limestone formed by the skeletons of animals too small to be seen without a magnifying lens.

Sandstones are made from grains of rock cemented together over time. The size and color of the grains of sandstone depend upon where they formed and how long the grains were weathered by wind or water before they formed rock. Sandstones can be many different colors, including red, black, and tan, depending upon where they formed. The rocks that make up the Grand Canyon are weathered layers of limestone and sandstone.

Grand Canyon National Park, Arizona

Conglomerates are sedimentary rocks that have pebbles and large fragments of other kinds of rocks cemented together by finer sand particles. Conglomerates are formed by moving waters such as the crashing surf on beaches and rapidly flowing large rivers. The energy of the rushing water moves the rocks around

Pyrite

and rounds them off. They become cemented together after they are buried beneath the sand. Quartz conglomerate rocks have large pieces of quartz set into fine grains of sandstone.

Breccia, like conglomerate, contains large pieces of different

Breccia

rocks and minerals. But unlike conglomerate, where the pieces of rock have been eroded and rounded, breccias contain large fragments that are sharp and angular and have not been eroded. **Fossils** are not common in this rock. Breccia is often found at the bottom of cliffs, close to where they crumbled and fell.

Another common kind of sedimentary rock is called shale, or mudstone. This is a fine-grained rock that forms from particles of clay. The grain size

Shale

in these rocks is so fine that the grains cannot be seen without a powerful microscope. Some pieces of shale contain fossilized ancient shelled animals such as mollusks.

Some kinds of rock don't come directly from molten rock or from sediments. They may look something like rocks in those groups, but they have changed in some ways. They are called **metamorphic rocks**, rocks that have changed their form.

Marble

In some metamorphic rocks, new minerals have formed over many years because of great heat and pressure. These metamorphic rocks look much different than the rocks from which they formed. Other metamorphic rocks hardly change at all in appearance from what they looked like before.

Green marble

You can think of igneous rocks as the first, or parent, rocks on Earth's crust. When igneous rocks weather, they break into smaller pieces that may be deposited and form sedimentary rocks. Both kinds may be changed under heat and pressure into metamorphic rocks.

Some types of marbles are fine grained, while others have larger grains. Marble can be polished beautifully smooth and is often used as a building stone. Marble with different color specks is made from limestone containing other kinds of mineral grains.

White marble columns

Slate is a metamorphic rock that formed from shale under high pressure inside the crust. Shale is sometimes squeezed so hard by movements in Earth's crust that its minerals form into layers of crystals that change the shale into slate. Slate is much harder and smoother than shale. It can be split into thin sheets that are used as roof tiles or as chalkboards in classrooms. Slate may be black, green, red, or purple. With high heat inside the crust, shale itself can be changed into another metamorphic rock called hornfels.

Slate roof

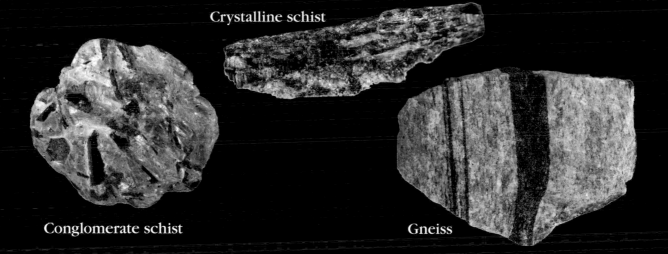

Crystalline schist

Conglomerate schist

Gneiss

Schist is another kind of metamorphic rock that can form from shale, slate, or basalt. Schist is often named after its most common mineral. It is a flaky rock and forms in layers. Mica schist is a common kind that contains flakes of mica. Other kinds of schist are talc, quartz, and hornblende schists.

Two other common metamorphic rocks are quartzite and gneiss. Quartzite is a heavy, tough rock that came from sandstone. Quartzite is the same color as the original sandstone—white, red, or brown. Gneiss can come from many different rocks. It usually has large crystals and bands. Gneiss often has mica and another mineral in alternate bands. The layers may be bent or irregular if the rock has formed under changing heat and pressure.

29

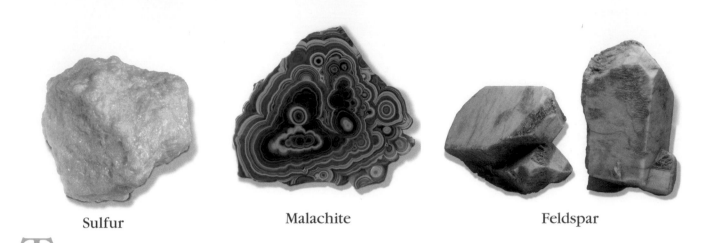

Sulfur   Malachite   Feldspar

Telling one mineral from another is something like guessing the villain in a mystery story. One clue may not be enough, but as the clues build up, the identity of the criminal becomes clearer. In much the same way, one property of a mineral may not be enough to identify it, but as you find out more properties you can usually identify the mineral.

Color is the most obvious property in helping to identify some minerals, but it may be the least reliable. Just a tiny trace of a chemical may change a mineral to a completely different color. For example, pure quartz is colorless and looks like glass. But some kinds of quartz are violet, rose, smoky, milky, green, black, or even banded with different colors, depending upon which chemicals they contain. Still, color can help in identifying some minerals. Minerals containing copper are often green like malachite or blue like azurite. Sulfur is yellow, calcite is usually white, and cinnabar is reddish. Use color as your first clue, but remember it is usually not enough to identify a mineral.

Streak is a better clue than color. To make a streak, you rub the mineral against a streak plate, a piece of unglazed porcelain such as the back of a bathroom tile. This leaves a powder trace of the mineral that looks different from the surface color. Gold leaves a yellow streak, but iron pyrite, which looks yellowish like gold, leaves a black streak. Dark minerals will sometimes leave a much lighter streak. Biotite mica, for example, looks dark but leaves a colorless streak.

Pyrite streak

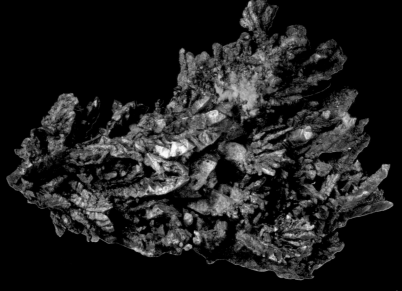

Metallic silver

Luster is another clue to help identify a mineral. You can easily tell a mineral's luster just by looking at it. Luster is the way a mineral shines in a beam of light. Some minerals have a metallic luster, and they shine like metals. Examples of minerals with this kind of luster are galena (lead), pyrite, gold, and silver. Nonmetallic lusters have different names such as glassy (quartz), sparkling (diamond), dull (chalk, clay), silky (asbestos), or pearly (talc).

Glassy quartz

Sparkling diamond

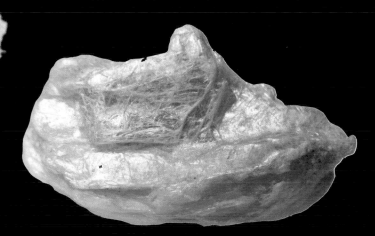

Silky asbestos

Pearly talc

Volcanic rock and obsidian flow in Deschutes National Forest, Oregon

Cleavage and **fracture** describe the way a mineral breaks. Most minerals fracture roughly or irregularly, but some cleave smoothly along a flat, even surface. Some minerals, such as quartz and glass, show a rounded fracture called conchoidal, which means "shell-shaped." Minerals can cleave in one direction or in several. Mica splits in one direction, feldspar splits in two directions that meet at nearly a right angle, and halite (rock salt) splits in three directions and forms cubes. Cleavage is not an easy property to judge, but it may help you in identifying one or another mineral.

Hardness is a property of minerals for which you have to test. Hardness does not mean how difficult or easy it is to break a mineral apart. For a geologist, hardness is a measure of how easily a mineral can scratch or be scratched. If you scratch a mineral against a substance of known hardness, the harder one will leave a scratch mark on the softer one.

The easiest and most common way to tell the hardness of a mineral is to use a scale described many years ago by a scientist name Friedrich Mohs. The Mohs hardness scale uses ten different minerals, from the softest, talc (1), to the hardest, diamond (10). With the exception of diamond, most of the minerals are common and not expensive.

| Talc | Gypsum | Calcite | Fluorite | Apatite |

Any mineral will scratch any other mineral with a lower number. If two minerals are equal in number, they won't easily scratch each other. Here's an easy way for you to test a mineral you find for hardness: Your fingernail can scratch 1 and 2. A penny can scratch 3. A steel knife can easily scratch 4 and can barely scratch 5. A steel knife can be scratched by 6. Glass can be scratched by 7. Quartz can be scratched by 8 or harder. It's not a good idea to use a diamond to test because it's way too expensive to risk scratching.

Feldspar Orthoclase	Quartz	Topaz	Corundum	Diamond	
6	7	8	9	10	HARDEST

It's a good idea to plan ahead before you go rock collecting. Always go with a responsible adult or family member. It's sensible to wear old clothes and sturdy, comfortable shoes. Even in the summer, it's best to wear long pants or slacks and a long-sleeve shirt. These will better protect your arms and legs against the sharp edges of rocks (not to mention protect against insect bites). One other item to consider bringing is a pair of plastic protective **goggles** to slip over your eyes or glasses when hammering a rock.

The first thing you'll need is a hammer with a hard steel head and a steel handle. You may not need a hammer if you're just collecting loose rocks, but even loose rocks may be too big to collect unless you break them apart. Next, bring along a sack made of strong material and some old newspapers to wrap each specimen. A magnifying lens for looking at small crystals and a pocketknife for testing hardness may also come in handy.

Young geologist studying rock

Bring a notebook or a smartphone or tablet to write down the number of the rock (start with number 1), where you found it, and the date. Write down any other observations you make. Mark each rock with a marking pencil or a number on adhesive tape. Start collecting in easy places where rocks have been broken before, such as an old open mine. Remember to ask permission before collecting on private property. Only collect what you are likely to use or to trade. Be conservation minded even when collecting what seems to be an endless supply of rocks.

Geologists studying graphical display
of oil and gas bearing on rocks

There's a difference between having a bunch of rocks and minerals in a drawer or a sack and having a rock collection. In a rock collection, each rock or mineral is labeled and identified. It's more fun having even a few rocks and minerals in an organized collection that you're making than having a big pile of jumbled rocks that you don't know anything about.

Try to look over and identify the rocks and minerals you collect as soon as possible when you get home. Except for a few minerals (such as rock salt), wash each one carefully in soapy water. Rub off loose material with a bristle brush. Be sure each specimen has a freshly broken side for easier identification. Wait till they dry and then try to identify each one. Use the labeled photos of rocks and minerals in this book to help you. Also use one of the websites suggested on page 48 to help identify your finds. Label each specimen with a number and put the same number in a file you make in a notebook or on a computer or tablet.

Set up your collection in plastic egg boxes for smaller specimens or plastic shoeboxes for larger ones. Use heavy cardboard to separate each box into the right-size squares. Small crystals and delicate specimens can be mounted on cotton balls. Minerals that flake easily can be sprayed with a clear plastic acrylic (you can get this at a hardware store). This kind of collection can be shown to your class in school. Ask your teacher about it.

Besides collecting, there are many other things you can do if you become interested in rocks and minerals. Here are some ideas to get you started.

Look for rock-hound clubs in your area by searching on the internet. Also look for interesting places to collect nearby. Many clubs accept young members or have a junior division for people your age. There are hundreds of clubs listed around the world and in every state in the United States. There is probably one near you.

Visit museums that have rock and mineral collections and search for rock and mineral stores online. Look for ideas about how to display your own rocks at home.

The rounded pebbles you find on the seashore or in riverbeds are polished by nature over hundreds of years. But you can polish them in a much shorter time at home. To do this you need a rock tumbler. These are machines that use an electric motor to tumble rocks over and over again in a small rubber container. You can find rock tumblers for sale in rock and mineral stores or on the internet. Tumbling produces beautiful gemlike rocks and minerals. You can use them just to display or to make jewelry.

Some rock hounds collect fossils. Fossils are the remains of animals or plants that have been preserved in rock for thousands of years. Most fossils are found in sedimentary rocks that were formed in the sediments of a sea, lake, or swamp. Find the best places to look for these from the members of a rock club in your area. Take a magnifying lens with you; many fossils are small and hard to see.

Every day of our lives we use many kinds of rocks and minerals, such as metals in pots and pans and in cars and trains, ceramics in cups and dishes, and products refined from petroleum, such as fuel, plastics, and rubber. And that's only a small sample of the many ways we use minerals daily. Scientists estimate that every person in the United States will use more than 3 million pounds of rocks and minerals during their lifetime.

There are rocks all around you everywhere you go. Even a common rock that you find outside your door may have formed millions and millions of years ago. Every rock and mineral is a bit of our planet's long history. You, as a rock hound, are not just a rock explorer but also a historian.

Amethyst

Malachite

Quartz

Feldspar

Mica

Calcite

Diamond

Emerald

Aquamarine

Ruby

Sapphire

Meteorite

Obsidian

Pyrite

Breccia

Asbestos

Slate

Marble

Chalcedony

Green marble

Crystalline schist

Conglomerate schist

Gneiss

Talc

Sulfur

Fluorite

Apatite

Topaz

Corundum

Gypsum

Shale

Silver

GLOSSARY

Cleavage—Splitting of a rock along definite planes.

Compounds—Made up of more than one mineral.

Core—The ball-shaped core that is beneath the crust and the mantle. It is mostly made up of iron and nickel. The core is split into two different zones, a molten outer core and a solid inner core.

Crust—The outermost layer of the planet. It is composed of igneous, metamorphic, and sedimentary rocks.

Crystal—A small piece of substance that has many sides and is formed when the substance turns into a solid.

Fossil—The remains or impression of a once living thing.

Fracture—The general appearance of a broken surface of a rock.

Geologist—A scientist who studies rocks, minerals, layers of soil, land formation, and more in order to learn about the history of the Earth.

Goggles—Protective eyeglasses that fit over your face and that are worn to protect your eyes.

Hardness—The scratch resistance of a mineral determined by its capacity to scratch or be scratched by another mineral.

Igneous rocks—Rocks formed by solidification of magma.

Lava—Melted rock from a volcano.

Luster—A glow of reflected light.

Magma—Hot liquid rock below the surface of the Earth.

Mantle—The layer between the crust and the core. It is composed mostly of peridotite and is very dense. The mantle is divided into the upper mantle and lower mantle.

Metamorphic rocks—Rocks that have changed over time due to extreme pressure and heat.

Meteor—A piece of rock or metal that burns and glows brightly in the sky as it falls from outer space into the Earth's atmosphere.

Meteorite—A piece of rock or metal from outer space that reaches the surface of the Earth without burning up entirely.

Mineral—A substance, such as quartz, that is naturally formed under the ground.

Mohs scale—A scale of hardness for minerals that ranges from a value of 1 for talc to 10 for diamond.

Rock hound—Someone who collects rocks.

Sedimentary rocks—Rocks formed by or from deposits of sediments, usually at the bottoms of lakes and oceans. Sediment can include minerals, small pieces of plants, and other organic matter.

Semiprecious—A gemstone that is not a diamond, ruby, emerald, or sapphire.

Streak—The color of the fine powder of a mineral obtained by scratching or rubbing against a hard surface, which reveals an important distinguishing character.

INDEX

Bold type indicates illustrations.

READ MORE ABOUT IT

Seymour Simon's website
www.seymoursimon.com

U.S. Geological Survey
pubs.usgs.gov/gip/collect1/
collectgip.html
education.usgs.gov/lessons/
schoolyard/RockDescription.html

American Federation of
Mineralogical Societies
www.amfed.org/kids.htm